FIGHTING FIRES

Nick Hunter

www.raintreepublishers.co.uk
Visit our website to find out more information about Raintree books.

To order:
☎ Phone 0845 6044371
▤ Fax +44 (0) 1865 312263
▣ Email myorders@raintreepublishers.co.uk

Customers from outside the UK please telephone +44 1865 312262

Raintree is an imprint of **Capstone Global Library Limited**, a company incorporated in England and Wales having its registered office at 7 Pilgrim Street, London, EC4V 6LB – Registered company number: 6695582.

Text © Capstone Global Library Limited 2012
First published in hardback in 2012

Edited by Dan Nunn, Rebecca Rissman, and Catherine Veitch
Designed by Joanne Malivoire
Picture research by Elizabeth Alexander
Originated by Capstone Global Library
Printed and bound in China by CTPS

ISBN 978 1 406 23207 3
15 14 13 12 11
10 9 8 7 6 5 4 3 2 1

British Library Cataloguing in Publication Data
Hunter, Nick.
Fighting fires. – (Heroic jobs)
363.3'781-dc22
A full catalogue record for this book is available from the British Library.

Acknowledgements
We would like to thank the following for permission to reproduce photographs: Getty Images pp. 7 (Eduardo Parra), 9 (David Allan Brandt), 14 (Jac Depczyk), 15 (Nigel Shuttleworth/Life File), 16 (Radius Images), 18 (Yoshikazu Tsuno/AFP), 19 (China Photos), 22–23 (William West/AFP), 26 (ChinaFotoPress), 29 (Patrick Strattner); p. 28 iStockphoto (© Edward Shaw); Photolibrary pp. 21 (Barrett & MacKay), 24 (Marijan Murat), 25 (INC SUPERSTOCK), 27 (Jacques Loic); Shutterstock pp. 4 (© Monkey Business Images), 5 (© Patricia Marks), 6 (© mikeledray), 8 (© Kazela), 10 (© Four Oaks), 11 (© riganmc), 12 (© Dariush M.), 13 (© John Sartin), 17 (© Keith Muratori), 20 (© Carlos Neto).

Cover photograph of firefighters battling a house fire reproduced by permission of Photolibrary (Bill Stormont/Flint Collection).

Every effort has been made to contact copyright holders of material reproduced in this book. Any omissions will be rectified in subsequent printings if notice is given to the publisher.

We would like to thank Mark Oddi for his invaluable help in the preparation of this book.

Some words are shown in bold, **like this**. You can find out what they mean by looking in the glossary.

Contents

Fire!

The **alarm** bell rings at the fire station. Somewhere in the city, a building is on fire. The firefighters are ready to go. They slide down a pole to get to the fire engine. The driver starts up the engine and they're on their way.

Meet the firefighters

Firefighters have to keep fit and train hard to put out different types of fire. They have to be ready to rescue people. Firefighters risk their lives every day.

Did you know?

Firefighters deal with many different types of fire:
- fires in buildings
- fires in cars and other **vehicles**
- fires in forests and grasslands.

Fighting fires

Firefighters spray water or **foam** on a fire to put it out. Fire needs air to spread. Foam works by stopping air from reaching the fire.

Did you know?
Firefighters wear special equipment to help them **breathe** when inside smoke-filled buildings. Breathing in smoke is the main reason people die in fires.

9

Dangers of firefighting

A large fire can be very hot. Firefighters are in danger of being **burned** by the fire. Fire can also move very quickly and cause burning buildings to collapse. Firefighters have to be careful not to get trapped.

A fire has destroyed this house.

Teamwork

Firefighters know that their job is dangerous. They work as a team to keep each other safe. Different team members do different jobs. Some team members operate the hose. Others rescue people from the fire.

Firefighters use radios to talk to their team.

radio

13

Fire engines

Fire engines sound a long, loud warning sound, or **siren**, to tell people that a fire engine is on its way. The fire engine carries the firefighters, their tools, and water to put out the fire.

Did you know?
The tallest ladder on a fire engine can reach over 30 metres high. That's about as high as four two-storey houses on top of each other.

Fire equipment

Firefighters wear tough, heavy clothing to protect them. Without this clothing, they would be burned by the heat of the fire. A helmet protects the firefighter's head.

helmet

protective jacket

Did you know?
A tank full of air helps a firefighter to **breathe** in a fire. It is connected to a mask covering their mouth and nose.

Fires in the city

City fires can start in factories, shops, or tall buildings. Fire engines race through busy streets to get to the fire. Ladders reach up to rescue people from the windows of the buildings.

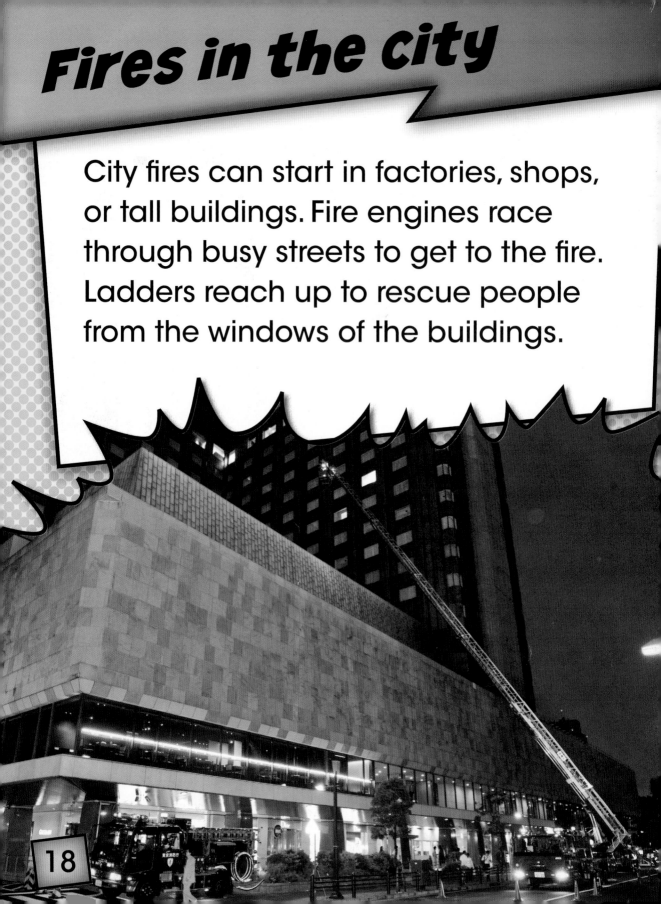

Did you know?
In 2010, more than 60 fire crews fought to put out a fire in a tower block in Shanghai, China. Many people were killed.

Fighting forest fires

Some of the biggest fires are in forests and grasslands. Dry wood and plants **burn** easily and forest fires spread quickly. Tiny flames, or **sparks**, are carried by the wind. These sparks can start new fires.

parachute

Did you know?
Sometimes special firefighters called smoke jumpers parachute into the middle of burning forests to put out fires.

Victoria, Australia, 2009

In Australia, forest fires are called bush fires. Bush fires raged across the state of Victoria in February 2009. Thousands of firefighters fought the huge flames. Whole towns were burned to the ground and many people were killed.

Special firefighters

Some firefighters are trained to do special jobs. Airport fire crews are always ready in case a plane has an accident. Planes carry lots of fuel, which can create a huge, very hot fire. Firefighters have to work fast to rescue the passengers.

Some firefighters use boats instead of fire engines to put out fires on board ships.

Becoming a firefighter

To become a firefighter you have to be strong and smart. Training will help you to understand how fires start and how they spread. Firefighters have to be very brave. They risk their lives to rescue others.

Firefighters train in all kinds of weather to keep fit.

Firefighters have to move quickly and work as a team.

Fire safety

The best way to help firefighters is to stop fires from starting. Here are some things you can do:

- Never play with matches or candles.
- Make sure your house has **smoke alarms**.
- Test smoke alarms once a week.

If you spot a fire, never try to put it out yourself. Get out, telephone the fire service, and stay out.

Did you know?
Fire services have different telephone numbers around the world:
- Australia: 000
- most of Europe: 112
- UK: 999
- United States: 911

Glossary

alarm bell or siren that that alerts or warns people about something

breathe take air into the lungs. People and animals need to breathe to stay alive.

burn catch fire or be damaged by fire

foam substance used to put out fires. It stops air from reaching the fire.

siren long, loud warning sound

smoke alarm alarm that warns people if there is a fire by detecting smoke

spark tiny flame that can cause a fire to start

vehicle something that is used to transport people or things. A car is a vehicle.

Find out more

Books

At the Fire Station (Technology at Work), Louise and Richard Spilsbury (Raintree Publishers, 2009)

Call the Fire and Rescue Service (In an Emergency), Cath Senker (Franklin Watts, 2010)

What's It Like to Be a Firefighter? Elizabeth Dowen and Lisa Thompson (A & C Black, 2010)

Websites

kids.nationalgeographic.com/kids/stories/peopleplaces/firefighter/
Tells you about the life of a typical firefighter and what it takes to become one.

www.firesafetyforkids.org
Information, games, and activities related to fire safety.

Index